IN THE

FOOTSTEPS

OF

JESUS

IN THE

FOOTSTEPS

OF

JESUS

MAX LUCADO

TYNDALE HOUSE PUBLISHERS, INC.

WHEATON, ILLINOIS

DESIGNED BY GLORIA CHANTELL

TITLE PAGE MOSAIC, USED BY PERMISSION; HAGIA SOPHIA MUSEUM, ISTANBUL, TURKEY.

PHOTOGRAPHY COURTESY OF BARRY BEITZEL

PRINTED IN U.S.A.

ISBN 0-8423-3910-8

04	03	02	01	00
5	4	3	2	1

CONTENTS

THE
ABUNDANT
HEART OF
GOD

4

Show me the path

where I should walk,

O Lord;

point out the right road for me to follow.

Lead me by your truth and teach me,

for you are the God who saves me.

All day long I put my hope in you.

PSALM 25:4-5

When Jesus says, "Come to me," he doesn't say come to religion, come to a system, or come to a doctrine. He gives you a very personal invitation to a God, an invitation to a Savior.

FATHER, HAD YOU NOT BECOME FLESH AND DWELT

AMONG US, HAD YOU NOT TREATED US WITH MERCY AND

KINDNESS, HAD YOU NOT LOVED US BEYOND OUR WORTH,

YOU'D STILL BE GOD. YOU'D STILL BE WORTHY OF OUR

PRAISE. AND YOU'D STILL BE HOLY. YET, FATHER, YOU DID

ALL OF THAT AND MORE.

Amen! Blessing and glory and wisdom and thanksgiving and honor
and power and strength belong to our God forever and forever. Amen!

REVELATION 7:12

6

7

WHEN YOU HURT, GOD HURTS WITH YOU. WHEN NO ONE

LISTENS TO YOU, GOD LISTENS TO YOU. WHEN YOU WIPE AWAY

TEARS OF LONELINESS OR FRUSTRATION OR ANGUISH, IN HEAVEN

THERE'S A PIERCED HAND APPROACHING A HEAVENLY FACE

8

WIPING AWAY A TEAR.

Jesus Christ . . .

is the faithful witness to these

things, the first to rise from the

dead, and the commander of all

the rulers of the world. All

praise to him who loves us and

has freed us from our sins by

shedding his blood for us.

REVELATION 1:5

LEARNING HOW TO TRUST GOD DEFINES THE MEANING

OF CHRISTIAN LIVING. GOD DOESN'T WAIT UNTIL

WE HAVE OUR MORAL LIFE IN ORDER BEFORE HE

STARTS LOVING US. THIS IS THE INEXPRESSIBLE

LOVE OF GOD.

ASHKELON

I myself no longer live, but Christ lives in me. So I live my life in this earthly body by trusting in the Son of God, who loved me and gave himself for me.

GALATIANS 2:20

11

WE HAVE BEEN TOUCHED
BY GOD'S TENDERNESS,
THE TENDERNESS OF A GENTLE
FATHER. HE DOESN'T COME
QUARRELING AND WRANGLING
AND FORCING HIS WAY INTO
ANYONE'S HEART. HE COMES INTO
OUR HEARTS LIKE A GENTLE
LAMB, NOT A ROARING LION.

He will feed his flock like a shepherd. He will carry the lambs in his arms, holding them close to his heart. He will gently lead the mother sheep with their young.

ISAIAH 40:11

13

WE SERVE THE GOD WHO DESIGNED THE UNIVERSE AND

SET OUR WORLD IN MOTION. BUT THOSE HANDS

THAT HUNG THE STARS IN THE HEAVENS ALSO WIPED

AWAY THE TEARS OF THE WIDOW AND THE LEPER.

AND THEY WILL WIPE AWAY YOUR TEARS AS WELL.

I am leaving you with a gift—

peace of mind and heart.

15

And the peace I give isn't like the peace the world gives.

So don't be troubled or afraid.

JOHN 14:27

WHERE IS GOD WHEN WE HURT? WHERE IS HE WHEN SLEEP WON'T COME? WHERE IS HE WHEN WE AWAKEN IN A HOSPITAL BED WITH PAIN THAT WON'T SUBSIDE? HE'S RIGHT HERE! HE HUNG ON THE GALLOWS TO PROVE ONCE AND FOR ALL—WITH PIERCED HANDS AND BLOOD-STAINED FACE— THAT HE'S HERE. HE DIDN'T CREATE THE HURT; HE CAME TO TAKE IT AWAY.

16

BETH-GUVRIN

Dear friends, don't be surprised
at the fiery trials you are
going through, as if something
strange were happening to
you. Instead, be very glad—
because these trials will make
you partners with Christ in his
suffering, and afterward you
will have the wonderful joy of
sharing his glory when it is
displayed to all the world.

1 PETER 4:12-13

17

OUR GOD IS NOT ALOOF. HE'S NOT SO FAR ABOVE US THAT

HE CAN'T SEE AND UNDERSTAND OUR PROBLEMS.

JESUS ISN'T A GOD WHO STAYED ON THE MOUNTAINTOP—

HE'S A SAVIOR WHO CAME DOWN AND LIVED AND

WORKED WITH THE PEOPLE. EVERYWHERE HE WENT,

THE CROWDS FOLLOWED, DRAWN TOGETHER BY

THE MAGNET THAT WAS—AND IS—THE SAVIOR.

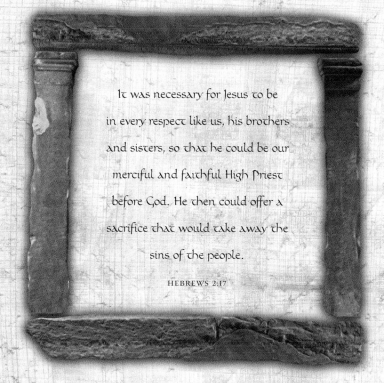

It was necessary for Jesus to be
in every respect like us, his brothers
and sisters, so that he could be our
merciful and faithful High Priest
before God. He then could offer a
sacrifice that would take away the
sins of the people.

HEBREWS 2:17

THE LOVE OF CHRIST COMPELS US TO DO WHAT

WE THOUGHT WE NEVER COULD DO AND GO

TO HEIGHTS WE THOUGHT WE NEVER COULD REACH.

PRECIOUS IS THE NAME OF JESUS!

Whom have I in heaven but you? I desire you more than anything on earth.

PSALM 73:25

GOD'S GREATEST DREAM IS
FOR YOU TO GO TO HEAVEN—
HIS PRIORITY IS TO GET YOU
INTO HIS KINGDOM. AND YET,
THOUGH HE IS SOVEREIGN,
HE NEVER FORCES HIS WILL
ON ANY HUMAN BEING—
HE SIMPLY WAITS ON YOUR
ACKNOWLEDGMENT OF HIM
AS LORD.

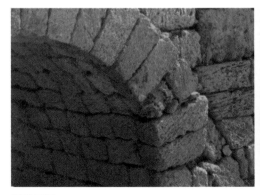

CAESAREA

THE LORD ISN'T REALLY BEING SLOW

ABOUT HIS PROMISE TO RETURN,

AS SOME PEOPLE THINK. NO, HE IS

BEING PATIENT FOR YOUR SAKE.

HE DOES NOT WANT ANYONE TO

PERISH, SO HE IS GIVING MORE TIME

FOR EVERYONE TO REPENT. 2 PETER 3:9

LED
BY HIS
LOVE

I command you—be strong and courageous! Do not be afraid or discouraged. For the LORD your God is with you wherever you go.

JOSHUA 1:9

26

GOD NEVER TURNS HIS BACK ON THOSE WHO ASK HONEST QUESTIONS. IF YOU ARE ASKING HONEST QUESTIONS OF GOD, HE WILL NOT TURN AWAY FROM YOU.

FATHER, WE LOOK AT YOUR PLAN AND SEE THAT IT'S BASED

ON LOVE. IT'S NOT DETERMINED BY OUR PERFORMANCE.

WE PRAY YOU'LL HELP US UNDERSTAND WHAT IT MEANS TO

BE CAPTIVATED BY YOUR LOVE . . . TO BE OVERWHELMED BY

YOUR GRACE . . . TO COME HOME TO YOU ON THE BEAUTIFUL

PATH THAT YOU'VE ALREADY CARVED OUT FOR US.

We know that the Son of God has come, and he has given us understanding so that we can know the true God. And now we are in God because we are in his Son, Jesus Christ. He is the only true God, and he is eternal life.

1 JOHN 5:20

WADI
FARIA

GOD IS WITH YOU. GOD IS WITH YOU! THE SAME GOD

WHO GUIDED HIS SON THROUGH DEATH AND BACK TO LIFE

MADE THIS PROMISE: HE WILL NEVER LEAVE YOU OR FORSAKE

YOU. HE IS RIGHT THERE WITH YOU, PERHAPS EVEN MORE IN

TIMES OF CRISIS THAN ANY OTHER TIME.

The LORD is righteous in
everything he does; he is filled
with kindness.

PSALM 145:17

You don't need a translator to help you

understand the language of God's heart.

You have his Word, his simple gospel. You need

only to listen, to keep your heart open to

his. Let God be your spiritual guide.

He is our God forever and
ever, and he will be our
guide until we die.

PSALM 48:14

33

CAESAREA

FATHER, WE INVITE YOU TO BE OUR GUIDE THROUGH LIFE. LORD, WE DON'T ASK THAT YOU TAKE FROM US THE WORRIES OF THIS LIFE BUT THAT YOU SURFACE THE WORRIES OF THIS LIFE SO THAT WE CAN SHARE THEM WITH YOU AND TURN THEM OVER TO YOU.

The LORD your God has arrived to live among you. He is a mighty savior. He will rejoice over you with great gladness. With his love, he will calm all your fears. He will exult over you by singing a happy song.

ZEPHANIAH 3:17

35

IN THIS FAST-PACED WORLD IN WHICH WE LIVE, THE VERY

THING WE NEED TO DO IS WHAT WE OFTEN DON'T DO:

WE NEED SIMPLY TO SIT STILL AND OPEN OUR HEARTS TO THE

COUNSEL OF GOD. THEN WE WILL BE WELL PREPARED

FOR WHATEVER THE DAY BRINGS.

Surely the godly are praising your name,

for they will live in your presence.

PSALM 140:13

JUST AS A NAVIGATOR CAN'T FIND HIS DESTINATION WITHOUT A COMPASS, WE CAN'T FIND PEACE WITHOUT GOD'S COMPASS—THE WORD OF TRUTH.

38

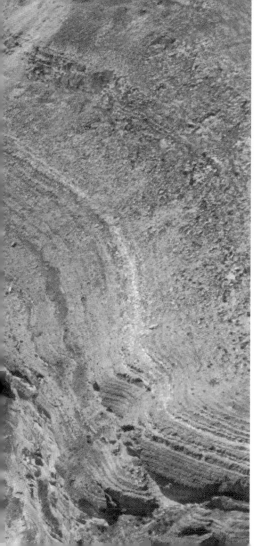

ST. GEORGES MONASTERY,
JUDEAN WILDERNESS

Make them pure and holy
by teaching them your
words of truth.

JOHN 17:17

YOUR LIFE CAME WITH AN OWNER'S MANUAL—

IF YOU FOLLOW THE TEACHINGS IN IT,

40

YOU WILL BE FULLY EQUIPPED AND YOUR LIFE WILL

OPERATE MUCH MORE SMOOTHLY.

Such things were written
in the Scriptures long ago to
teach us. They give us hope and
encouragement as we wait
patiently for God's promises.

ROMANS 15:4

41

SEVERAL HUNDRED YEARS BEFORE JESUS, ISAIAH SAID THAT THERE IS ONE WHO IS CHOSEN; THERE IS ONE WHO IS PROMISED. HE SAID THAT SOMETHING WOULD HAPPEN TO CONVINCE US THAT WE'RE NOT SPINNING IN A WHIRLPOOL HEADED TOWARD NOWHERE, BUT WE'RE FLOATING DOWN THE RIVER OF ETERNITY GUIDED BY GOD.

This is what God has
testified: He has given us
eternal life, and this life
is in his Son.

1 JOHN 5:11

44

LORD, HELP US SEARCH YOUR WORD FOR PRACTICAL HELP IN OUR DAILY LIVES. HELP US TO LEAN ON YOU, AND HELP US TURN FIRST TO YOU. GIVE US, FATHER, YOUR STRENGTH AND GUIDANCE, INCREASE OUR HOPE, AND MULTIPLY OUR FAITH.

TEACH ME TO DO YOUR WILL,
FOR YOU ARE MY GOD. MAY
YOUR GRACIOUS SPIRIT LEAD ME
FORWARD ON A FIRM FOOTING.

PSALM 143:10

STRENGTH
ALONG THE
WAY

48

The LORD is my strength,

my shield from every danger.

I trust in him with all my heart.

He helps me, and my heart is filled

with joy. I burst out in songs

of thanksgiving.

PSALM 28:7

GOD DOES NOT ABANDON HIS CHILDREN, ESPECIALLY IN TIMES OF STRUGGLE. HE PROMISES TO BE WITH YOU ALWAYS. ARE YOU TRYING TO TACKLE AN ATTITUDE OR PUT AWAY A BAD HABIT OR OVERCOME GUILT? YOU CAN'T SEE HIS POWER, BUT IT'S REAL—YOU'RE NOT ALONE.

THE POWER THAT LIVES IN GOD'S CHILDREN IS THE SAME

POWER THAT WAS PRESENT AT THE CREATION, CALLING

INTO BEING THIS EXISTENCE THAT WE CALL THE WORLD.

THAT SAME POWER IS ALIVE TODAY TO CONVINCE YOU,

CONVICT YOU, EQUIP YOU, AND ENCOURAGE YOU.

He made the earth by his power, and he preserves it by his wisdom.
He has stretched out the heavens by his understanding.

JEREMIAH 51:15

51

BELVOIR
CASTLE

GOD'S POWER IS UNLEASHED WHEN

GOD'S PEOPLE INTERCEDE.

52

The earnest prayer of a
righteous person has great
power and wonderful results.

JAMES 5:16

As long as we have hope, as long as we recognize

that this world is not our home, as long

as we recognize that someday all of our problems

will be solved, we will have found our

source of strength.

55

The Sovereign LORD is my
strength! He will make me as
surefooted as a deer and bring
me safely over the mountains.

HABAKKUK 3:19

ON'T HURRY GOD. THE PROBLEMS THAT WE THINK MAY DROWN US TODAY COULD BE THE VERY STEPPING-STONES TO GREATER SPIRITUAL STRENGTH TOMORROW. THROUGHOUT SCRIPTURE WE ARE REMINDED TO BE PATIENT IN SUFFERING, IN PHYSICAL DISTRESS, IN EMOTIONAL DISCOURAGEMENT. THE FATHER WILL SUPPLY OUR NEEDS. DON'T HURRY GOD.

Commit everything you do to the LORD. Trust

him, and he will help you.

PSALM 37:5

57

FATHER, YOU PROMISED THAT THERE WOULD BE FAITH AND

STRENGTH AND HOPE TO MEET LIFE'S PROBLEMS.

FATHER, GIVE THAT STRENGTH TO THOSE WHOSE ANXIETIES

HAVE BURIED THEIR DREAMS, WHOSE ILLNESSES HAVE

HOSPITALIZED THEIR HOPES, WHOSE BURDENS ARE BIGGER

THAN THEIR SHOULDERS.

LORD, don't hold back your tender mercies from me.

My only hope is in your unfailing love and faithfulness.

PSALM 40:11

EACH STATEMENT MADE BY JESUS ON THE CROSS IS LIKE A POST THAT WE SEE SOMETIMES ON THE SIDE OF THE ROAD THAT READS "POWER LINE BURIED HERE." IF YOU DIG DOWN, SURE ENOUGH, YOU'RE GOING TO STRIKE POWER. THOSE WORDS OF CHRIST ARE A SOURCE OF ENERGY INTO WHICH ALL OF US CAN TAP.

SAMARIA

61

I am the resurrection and the life. Those who believe in me, even though they die like everyone else, will live again.

JOHN 11:25

THE MOST POWERFUL LIFE IS THE MOST SIMPLE LIFE.

THE MOST POWERFUL LIFE IS THE LIFE THAT KNOWS

62   WHERE IT'S GOING, KNOWS ITS SOURCE OF STRENGTH,

AND STAYS FREE OF CLUTTER AND HAPPENSTANCE

AND HURRIEDNESS.

You won't spend the rest of
your life chasing after evil desires,
but you will be anxious to do
the will of God.

1 PETER 4:2

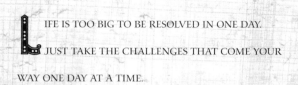

LIFE IS TOO BIG TO BE RESOLVED IN ONE DAY. JUST TAKE THE CHALLENGES THAT COME YOUR WAY ONE DAY AT A TIME.

O my Strength, to you I sing praises, for you, O God, are my refuge, the God who shows me unfailing love.

PSALM 59:17

YOU MAY LOOK AHEAD AND SEE

SOME CRISIS COMING DOWN

THE PIKE AND THINK, I'LL

NEVER BE ABLE TO HANDLE

THAT. YOU PROBABLY COULDN'T

RIGHT NOW, BUT GOD IS WITH

YOU, AND HE WILL GIVE YOU

THE STRENGTH YOU NEED.

CAPERNAUM

BLESS THE LORD, WHO IS MY ROCK.

HE GIVES ME STRENGTH FOR WAR

AND SKILL FOR BATTLE. HE IS MY

LOVING ALLY AND MY FORTRESS, MY

TOWER OF SAFETY, MY DELIVERER.

67

HE STANDS BEFORE ME AS A SHIELD,

AND I TAKE REFUGE IN HIM. HE SUB-

DUES THE NATIONS UNDER ME. PSALM 144:1-2

PRECIOUS

IN HIS

SIGHT

The LORD is slow
to anger and rich in
unfailing love,
forgiving every kind
of sin and rebellion.

NUMBERS 14:18

No matter what you do, no matter how far you fall, no matter how ugly you become, God has a relentless, undying, unfathomable, unquenchable love from which you cannot be separated. Ever!

A LOT OF US LIVE WITH A HIDDEN FEAR THAT GOD IS ANGRY AT US. SOMEWHERE, SOMETIME, SOME SUNDAY SCHOOL CLASS OR SOME TELEVISION SHOW CONVINCED US THAT GOD HAS A WHIP BEHIND HIS BACK, A PADDLE IN HIS BACK POCKET, AND HE'S GOING TO NAIL US WHEN WE'VE GONE TOO FAR. NO CONCEPT COULD BE MORE WRONG! YOUR SAVIOR'S FATHER IS VERY FOND OF YOU AND ONLY WANTS TO SHARE HIS LOVE WITH YOU.

The LORD is good. When trouble comes, he is a strong refuge. And he knows everyone who trusts in him.

NAHUM 1:7

EN-GEDI

I WONDER IF JESUS DOESN'T MUSTER UP A SLIGHT SMILE

AS HIS LOST SHEEP COME STRAGGLING INTO THE FOLD—

THE BEATEN, BROKEN, DIRTY SHEEP WHO STAND AT THE

DOOR LOOKING UP AT THE SHEPHERD ASKING, "CAN I COME

IN? I DON'T DESERVE IT, BUT IS THERE ROOM IN YOUR KING-

DOM FOR ONE MORE?" THE SHEPHERD LOOKS DOWN AT THE

SHEEP AND SAYS, "COME IN, THIS IS YOUR HOME."

You can be sure that the one
who brings that person back
will save that sinner from
death and bring about the
forgiveness of many sins.

JAMES 5:20

WHEN YOU WAKE UP AND LOOK IN THE MIRROR IN THE

MORNING, YOU'RE SEEING GOD'S POETRY. YOU

MAY THINK HE'S NOT MUCH OF A POET, BUT WHEN GOD

WOVE YOU TOGETHER, IT WAS NOT BY ACCIDENT,

IT WAS NOT HAPPENSTANCE, IT WAS NOT A MISTAKE. YOU

ARE THE RESULT OF ALL THE CREATIVE ENERGY OF

AN OMNIPOTENT, OMNIPRESENT, AND OMNISCIENT GOD

POURED INTO THE FORMATION OF HUMANITY.

DEAD SEA REGION

You made all the delicate, inner
parts of my body and knit me

77

together in my mother's womb.
Thank you for making me so
wonderfully complex! Your
workmanship is marvelous—
and how well I know it.

PSALM 139:13-14

Some facts will never change. One fact is that you are forgiven. If you are in Christ, when He sees you, your sins are covered—He doesn't see them. He sees you better than you see yourself. And that is a glorious fact of your life.

Everyone who believes in him will have their sins forgiven through his name.

ACTS 10:43

LORD, LET US NOT PRETEND TO BE SOMETHING WE'RE NOT.

YOU KNOW US EARLY IN THE MORNING; YOU KNOW

US LATE AT NIGHT. YOU KNOW US WHEN WE'RE WEAK;

YOU KNOW US WHEN WE'RE STRONG. FATHER, REMIND

US THAT YOU STILL CARE AND THAT YOU STILL LOVE US.

God is light

and there is no darkness in him at all.

1 JOHN 1:5

WHAT HAVE WE EVER DONE TO DESERVE THE HEALING TOUCH OF JESUS TO OUR SOULS? NOTHING! YET OFTEN WE COME TO JESUS FEELING PRETTY GOOD ABOUT OURSELVES, SAYING, "HEY, I'LL MAKE A GREAT CONTRIBUTION TO YOUR TEAM." HOGWASH! JESUS DOESN'T NEED US ON HIS TEAM. AND HE DOESN'T FORGIVE US ON THE BASIS OF WHAT WE'VE DONE. HE FORGIVES US ON THE BASIS OF WHO HE IS.

82

MASADA

83

Yes, the LORD has
done amazing things
for us! What joy!

PSALM 126:3

When Jesus told the story of the missing sheep,

some of the people knew how it felt to be

lost among the crowd. Jesus wanted us to

understand that we have a Father who sees

and cares for each one of his children—

that we are all equally valuable to him.

I am counting on the LORD;

yes, I am counting on him

I have put my hope in his word.

PSALM 130:5

85

OUR VALUE IS INHERENT—IT'S NOT BASED ON THE PH.D.
AFTER OUR NAME OR THE AMOUNT OF MONEY IN OUR BANK
ACCOUNT. WE HAVE VALUE SIMPLY BECAUSE WE ARE. IN THE EYES OF
GOD, EVERY HUMAN IS PRICELESS SIMPLY BECAUSE HE OR SHE IS THE
CREATION OF THE ALMIGHTY GOD.

You do not belong to yourself,
for God bought you with a
high price.

1 CORINTHIANS 6:19-20

88

THE GOSPELS ARE LIKE A
TAPESTRY, WOVEN TOGETHER
WITH TWO INCREDIBLE POINTS:
THE IMMEASURABLE VALUE OF
EACH PERSON AND THE
UNIMAGINABLE DEPTH OF
GOD'S GRACE.

I TRUST IN YOUR UNFAILING LOVE. I

WILL REJOICE BECAUSE YOU HAVE

RESCUED ME. I WILL SING TO THE

LORD BECAUSE HE HAS BEEN SO

GOOD TO ME. PSALM 13:5-6

PEACE BEYOND UNDERSTANDING

Encourage each other.

Live in harmony and peace.

Then the God of love and peace

will be with you.

2 CORINTHIANS 13:11

THOSE WHO CALL THEMSELVES
FOLLOWERS OF GOD NEED TO DEAL SERIOUSLY
WITH THE ISSUE OF PEACE: THERE WILL BE
PEACE ON EARTH ONLY WHEN THERE
IS PEACE BETWEEN MAN AND GOD. AFTER ALL,
THE PATTERN FOR PEACE COMES FROM HEAVEN
ITSELF—IN JESUS, WHO RECONCILED EARTH
TO GOD THROUGH THE CROSS.

COULD YOU USE SOME PEACE IN YOUR LIFE TODAY?

WHEN YOUR LIFE IS IN TURMOIL AND YOU WONDER IF

THERE WILL EVER BE ANOTHER PEACEFUL DAY FOR YOU,

OPEN YOUR HEART TO THE GOD OF PEACE AND TO JESUS,

THE PRINCE OF PEACE, AND TO THE HOLY SPIRIT, THE

LORD OF PEACE. THEY WILL ENVELOP YOU IN A PEACE

THAT TRANSCENDS UNDERSTANDING.

I have told you all this so that you may have peace in me.
Here on earth you will have many trials and sorrows.
But take heart, because I have overcome the world.

JOHN 16:33

95

IN THE MIDST OF YOUR BUSYNESS, THE CROSS IS STILL

THERE. IN THE MIDST OF YOUR EMPTINESS, THE CROSS IS

STILL THERE. THE PROMISES OF JESUS STILL STAND TODAY.

YOU CAN CLAIM PEACE IN THE MIDST OF A HECTIC LIFE—

NOT WITHOUT SACRIFICE, BUT YOU CAN DO IT.

LORD, you will grant us peace,

for all we have accomplished

is really from you.

ISAIAH 26:12

THAT PEACE THAT PASSES UNDERSTANDING CANNOT BE

OBTAINED IF WE SACRIFICE VALUABLE RELATIONSHIPS

AT THE EXPENSE OF FLEETING GRATIFICATIONS.

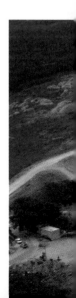

Live peaceably with each other.

1 THESSALONIANS 5:13

99

HAZOR

DO YOU FEEL YOU'VE SPENT YOUR LIFE IN ENDLESS PURSUIT OF CONTENTMENT? DO YOU REACH THE TOP OF THE LADDER AND DISCOVER YOU DON'T WANT TO BE THERE ANY-MORE? DO YOU DREAM ABOUT HAVING THE PERFECT MATE, AND ONCE YOU MARRY, YOU REALIZE HE OR SHE ISN'T PERFECT? CONTENTMENT IS NOT FOUND IN THINGS OF THIS WORLD; THE ONLY PATH TO CONTENTMENT IS THROUGH CHRIST.

Stop loving this evil world and all that it offers you,

for when you love the world, you show that you do not

have the love of the Father in you.

1 JOHN 2:15

Can you say to Jesus, "This burden's too heavy for me.

I want you to be my coworker. I want you to

carry this burden with me. I cannot do it any

longer"? If you will come to him, if you'll

allow him to carry that burden with you, he promises

that you will receive rest.

I have given rest to the weary

and joy to the sorrowing.

JEREMIAH 31:25

FATHER, AS YOU STILLED THE STORM ON THE SEA OF GALILEE, WILL YOU STILL THE STORMS THAT RAGE WITHIN OUR HEARTS? WILL YOU CALM THE WHIRLING WINDS OF FEAR AND HURT THAT THREATEN OUR FAITH? WILL YOU, FATHER, DRAW US EVER CLOSER TO YOU?

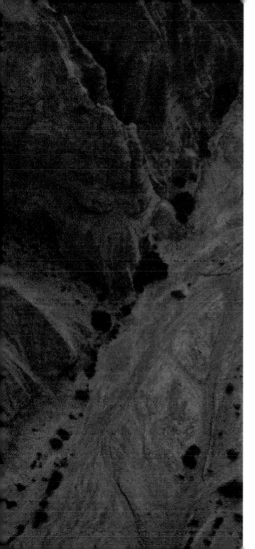

Jesus answered, "Why are you afraid? You have so little faith!" Then he stood up and rebuked the wind and waves, and suddenly all was calm.

MATTHEW 8:26

GOD OF PEACE, FATHER OF COMFORT, WE PRAY THAT YOUR

KINGDOM WOULD COME INTO OUR HEARTS AND

THAT PEACE WOULD RULE. TEACH US WHAT IT MEANS TO BE

PEACEMAKERS. HELP US CULTIVATE PEACE BETWEEN

OTHERS AND YOU—IN OUR NEIGHBORHOODS, OFFICES,

SCHOOLROOMS. TEACH US THE ART OF BUILDING

BRIDGES INSTEAD OF WALLS. WE GLORIFY YOUR NAME, THE

GREAT GOD OF PEACE.

How wonderful it is, how
pleasant, when brothers live
together in harmony!

PSALM 133:1

107

PEACE IS NEVER SOUGHT AT THE EXPENSE OF TRUTH.

GOD NEVER CALLS US INTO A RELATIONSHIP WITH HIM

JUST TO HAVE A RELATIONSHIP. HE SETS TRUTH IN FRONT OF

US AND SAYS, "AGREE TO THAT TRUTH AND THEN WE CAN

HAVE A RELATIONSHIP."

Unfailing love and truth have
met together. Righteousness
and peace have kissed!

PSALM 85:10

MAKE US, O GOD, INTO YOUR

PEACEMAKERS. GIVE US

COURAGE AS WE STAND ON

FIELDS OF DAILY CONFLICT.

LET US BE TOOLS OF

RECONCILIATION; LET US

BE AMBASSADORS OF LOVE;

110

LET US BE AS YOU ARE—

PEACEMAKERS, THAT WE

MAY BE CALLED THE CHILDREN

OF GOD.

SINAI

GOD BLESSES THOSE WHO WORK

FOR PEACE, FOR THEY WILL BE

CALLED THE CHILDREN OF GOD.

MATTHEW 5:9

FAITH
FOR REAL
LIFE

114

The LORD God is our light
and protector. He gives us grace
and glory. No good thing will the
LORD withhold from those
who do what is right.

PSALM 84:11

If God has been with you this far, he's not going to leave you during troubled times. Your faith has brought you this far. Hold on to your faith when the going gets tough.

We pray, O Father, that in the hours when we find ourselves in the dungeons of doubt, you would hear our questions. Forgive us for demanding that you answer our questions as we want them answered. Give us understanding. And, if we cannot understand, increase our trust in you.

I know, LORD, that a person's life is not his own. No one is able to plan his own course. So correct me, LORD, but please be gentle.

JEREMIAH 10:23-24

117

CAPERNAUM

HAS ANY GOOD EVER COME OUT OF WORRYING?

WORRY ONLY COMPARTMENTALIZES US AND PARALYZES

US, MAKING US UNABLE TO DO WHAT WE SET OUT TO DO.

IF WE ARE WORRIED ABOUT A PROBLEM, WE MUST SIMPLY

TRUST THE LORD.

When doubts filled my mind,

your comfort gave me renewed

hope and cheer.

PSALM 94:19

DON'T PUT YOUR HOPE INTO THINGS THAT CAN CHANGE:

RELATIONSHIPS, MONEY, TALENTS, BEAUTY, EVEN

120

HEALTH. SET YOUR SIGHTS ON THE ONE THING THAT CAN

NEVER CHANGE—TRUST IN YOUR HEAVENLY FATHER.

KEFR BARAM

I look to you for help,

O Sovereign LORD.

You are my refuge.

PSALM 141:8

121

REMEMBER THE LORD. REMEMBER WHO IS IN CONTROL. REMEMBER HIS GOODNESS IN THE PAST. REMEMBER GOD'S CLOSENESS IN THE PRESENT. REMEMBER HIS POWER FOR THE FUTURE.

I am with you always, even to the end of the age.

MATTHEW 28:20

MAKE YOUR FAITH AN INDEPENDENT, DOGGED FAITH,

FIRMLY PLANTED IN GOD'S SACRIFICED SON ON THE

HILL OF CALVARY. IT CAN NEVER BE TAKEN AWAY FROM YOU.

I will praise the LORD as long as I live.

I will sing praises to my God even with my dying breath.

PSALM 146:2

IF YOU HAVE NO FAITH IN THE FUTURE, THEN YOU HAVE NO POWER IN THE PRESENT. IF YOU HAVE NO FAITH IN THE LIFE BEYOND THIS LIFE, THEN YOUR PRESENT LIFE IS GOING TO BE POWER-LESS. BUT IF YOU BELIEVE IN THE FUTURE AND ARE ASSURED OF VICTORY, THEN THERE SHOULD BE A DANCE IN YOUR STEP AND A SMILE ON YOUR FACE.

Be careful how you live. . . .
Even if [your neighbors]
accuse you of doing wrong,
they will see your honorable
behavior, and they will
believe and give honor to
God when he comes to judge
the world.

1 PETER 2:12

127

ONE THING NO ONE CAN TAKE AWAY FROM YOU IS

YOUR FAITH. THIS WORLD CAN AND MAY TAKE

EVERYTHING YOU HAVE. BUT NO ONE CAN TAKE AWAY

YOUR FAITH. GRAB THAT FAITH; CLUTCH TIGHTLY

THAT ANCHOR OF THE SOUL.

Your reward for trusting him will be the salvation of your souls.

1 PETER 1:9

129

I T'S NOT HARD TO HAVE FAITH WHEN ALL OUR BILLS ARE

BEING PAID, OUR KIDS ARE HEALTHY, AND OUR MARRIAGES

ARE INTACT. IT'S NOT HARD TO HAVE FAITH WHEN GOD GIVES

US EVERYTHING WE WANT. THE TRUE TEST OF FAITH COMES

WHEN CIRCUMSTANCES ARE DIFFICULT, WHEN OUR TRAIN OF

HOPE GETS DERAILED.

If we are unfaithful, he
remains faithful, for he
cannot deny himself.

2 TIMOTHY 2:13

132

FATHER, WE WANT TO SEE
YOU AND KNOW YOU BETTER.
WE ASK YOU, FATHER, TO HELP
US SEE JESUS AND TO DEEPEN
OUR FAITH UPON SEEING HIM
MORE CLEARLY.

I AM THE ALPHA AND THE OMEGA—

THE BEGINNING AND THE END.

TO ALL WHO ARE THIRSTY I WILL

GIVE THE SPRINGS OF THE WATER OF

LIFE WITHOUT CHARGE! REVELATION 21:6

JOY IN

HIS

PRESENCE

136

Don't forget to show
hospitality to strangers,
for some who have done this have
entertained angels without
realizing it!

HEBREWS 13:2

HERE'S A SUGGESTION: WE SHOULD ALL WEAR ANTENNAS TO WORK, TO CHURCH, TO SCHOOL—ANTENNAS THAT PICK UP ON PEOPLE WHO SEEM OUT OF PLACE, WHOSE LONELINESS SHOWS. WHY NOT BE THE ONE TO APPROACH THESE FOLKS AND EXTEND FRIENDSHIP TO THEM? MAYBE YOU THINK THE LAST THING YOU NEED IS ANOTHER FRIEND. BUT FRIENDLINESS—HOSPITALITY—IS A VIRTUE THAT BRINGS AS MUCH JOY TO THE GIVER AS TO THE RECEIVER.

I'VE NOTICED THAT THOSE WHO SERVE GOD MOST

JOYFULLY ARE THE ONES WHO KNOW HIM MOST

PERSONALLY. THOSE WHO ARE QUICKEST TO SPEAK

ABOUT JESUS ARE THOSE WHO REALIZE HOW GREAT

HAS BEEN THEIR OWN REDEMPTION.

I pray that God, who gives you hope, will keep you happy and
full of peace as you believe in him. May you overflow with
hope through the power of the Holy Spirit.

ROMANS 15:13

139

ARAD

WHAT IS UNIQUE ABOUT THE KINGDOM OF GOD?

YOUR ASSURANCE OF VICTORY. YOU HAVE WON! YOU CAN

BE CERTAIN THAT YOU WILL SOMEDAY STAND BEFORE THE

THRONE OF GOD AND SEE THE KING OF KINGS. YOU ARE

ASSURED THAT SOMEDAY YOU WILL ENTER A WORLD

WHERE THERE WILL BE NO MORE PAIN, NO MORE TEARS,

NO MORE SORROW.

The Lord isn't really being slow about his promise to return, as some people think. No, he is being patient for your sake. He does not want anyone to perish, so he is giving more time for everyone to repent.

2 PETER 3:9

HAVING A SAVIOR IN CHRIST MEANS THAT THE

HOPELESS HAVE HOPE, THE DEAD HAVE LIFE, AND

THE ABANDONED HAVE A FATHER.

I am praying that you will really
put your generosity to work, for
in so doing you will come to an
understanding of all the good
things we can do for Christ.

PHILEMON 1:6

Jesus has come into our dark hearts and extended a hand—he has broken in from the outside by an act of God and has lifted us up. Spiritually, we are secure. We're dwelling in the highlands with him.

As we know Jesus better, his divine power gives us everything we need for living a godly life. He has called us to receive his own glory and goodness!

2 PETER 1:3

Do you wonder where you can go for encouragement

and motivation? Go back to that moment

when you first saw the love of Jesus Christ. Remember

the day when you were separated from Christ?

You knew only guilt and confusion and then—

a light. Someone opened a door and light came

into your darkness, and you said in your heart,

"I am redeemed!"

He declared us not guilty because of his great kindness.

147

And now we know that we will inherit eternal life.

TITUS 3:7

AN ITINERANT PREACHER FROM NAZARETH CAN DO SOMETHING FOR THE HURT THAT LINGERS IN YOUR HEART. PERHAPS YOU'RE TRYING TO REBUILD AN ESTRANGED RELATIONSHIP. MAYBE YOUR LOSSES OUTNUMBER YOUR WINS. MAYBE YOU'VE BEEN TRYING TO FIND GOD FOR LONGER THAN YOU CAN REMEMBER. THERE WAS SOMETHING ABOUT THIS GALILEAN PREACHER THAT MADE PEOPLE CLUSTER AROUND HIM LIKE HE WAS GOD'S GIFT TO HUMANITY. HE IS YOUR GIFT AS WELL.

148

CAESAREA (AQUEDUCT)

I am the light of the
world. If you follow me,
you won't be stumbling
through the darkness,
because you will have the
light that leads to life.

JOHN 8:12

149

Sometimes life doesn't seem fair, does it? Have you ever

wondered why good people have to hurt?

Why the innocent suffer? Often those who have been

most battered by life seem to understand Jesus

best. His assurance finds its way into the darkest

corners of life, because, regardless of our

circumstances, God meets our needs. By surrendering

to him, the ultimate victory is ours.

Don't say,

"I will get even for this

wrong." Wait for the LORD

to handle the matter.

PROVERBS 20:22

151

GOOD WILL TRIUMPH. GOD WILL WIN. THE FATE OF OUR ENEMY, SATAN, IS SEALED. WITH GOD AS OUR GUIDE, OUR DESTINATION IS HEAVEN. HALLELUJAH!

He who is the faithful witness
to all these things says,
"Yes, 1 am coming soon!"
Amen! Come, Lord Jesus!

REVELATION 22:20

RUN TO JESUS. JESUS WANTS
YOU TO GO TO HIM. HE
WANTS TO BECOME THE MOST
IMPORTANT PERSON IN YOUR
LIFE, THE GREATEST LOVE
YOU'LL EVER KNOW. HE
WANTS YOU TO LOVE HIM

154

SO MUCH THAT THERE'S NO
ROOM IN YOUR HEART AND
IN YOUR LIFE FOR SIN. INVITE
HIM TO TAKE UP RESIDENCE
IN YOUR HEART. DON'T WAIT
ANOTHER DAY.

SAMARIA

DEAR FRIENDS, IF OUR CONSCIENCE

IS CLEAR, WE CAN COME TO GOD

WITH BOLD CONFIDENCE. 1 JOHN 3:21

AMONG MAX LUCADO'S OTHER PUBLISHED WORKS ARE On the Anvil, No Wonder They Call Him the Savior, God Came Near, Six Hours One Friday, The Applause of Heaven, In the Eye of the Storm, And the Angels Were Silent, He Still Moves Stones, When God Whispers Your Name, A Gentle Thunder, In the Grip of Grace, God's Inspirational Promises, Cosmic Christmas, The Great House of God, Let the Journey Begin, The Cross, Just like Jesus, The Christmas Cross, The Gift for All People, When Christ Comes, Grace for the Moment, AND He Chose the Nails. HE HAS ALSO WRITTEN SEVERAL BOOKS FOR CHILDREN.